Haven't Lost My Dreams

Geoff Neville

Haven't Lost My Dreams

Haven't Lost My Dreams
ISBN 978 1 74027 023 6
Copyright © Geoff Neville 2000

First published 2000
Reprinted 2018

Ginninderra Press
PO Box 3461 Port Adelaide 5015 Australia
www.ginninderrapress.com.au

Contents

Grew Up on the Story	7
Mom Always Said	8
Leaving Home	10
You Don't Understand Him	13
A Letter Home	15
Old Bronc Saddle	16
No Bed of Roses	18
A Treasured Memory	19
Riding Broncs, Chasing Bulls	21
On the Road of Rodeo	22
Boy from the Bush, Girl from Town	24
Lonely Lady	25
Two Lonely People	26
Money Lost Or Won	27
Travel the Gravel	28
Stray Dog Like Me	30
Life Upon the Road	32
Rodeo Is What I Gotta Do	33
Rodeo Widow	35
The Aussie Battlers' Hymn	36
Keeping the Wolf from the Door	38
A Woman at Home	39
Haven't Lost My Dreams	40
A Lost Soul	41

Grew Up on the Story

I grew up on the story.
God made grass greener further out.
As a kid, I treasured every story told,
and the teller's truth was never in doubt.
I held in awe those tales of glory
to me those old-timers sold.

Sure,
>an' they'd tell of tall trees,
>mountain streams full of gold.
>Air sweeter than honey from busy bees
>and winter winds that were never cold.

There are
>mountains out yonder, smaller than sandhills,
>made for a small-town boy to climb.
>Country where time just stands still
>and good friends you'll always find.
>These were the stories told.

Yes.
>I grew up on the story,
>grass was greener further out.
>Life was a wonder for a boy
>and dreams had time to grow.
>I'd ride in the dust and glory
>where those old fellers wandered about.
>What a life for youth to enjoy
>and an adventurous soul to grow.

Mom Always Said

My mother always said,
'Don't go round with cowboys,
don't go fooling around with them,
you won't know where you're going,
and, boy, you never know where it'll end.'

It always made me wonder why
she would say those words,
as I ploughed the soil,
day in, day out, working their farm.

I dreamt of mustering herds,
droving overland where the bushman toil,
never thought being a cowboy
would bring me any harm.

'Twas rodeo time in town,
found myself a new friend,
Mom said to me,
'Stay away from cowboys,
you don't know where you're going,
and, boy, you never know where it'll end.'

Well, travelling is a disease,
burns deep in the heart.
Starts with a gentle squeeze,
and won't ever part.
You'll miss a meal with ease
while you learn this craft.

Mother always said,
'Don't go round with cowboys,
stay away from them,
it's a lonely place you're going,
boy, where the days they never end.'

You take to driving trucks,
picking fruit and calling home,
wherever you have the luck.
Across this wide land you roam,
each moment searching for a buck,
trying to reach a dream unknown.

My mother always said,
'Don't go following them,
cold 'n' hungry ain't no feather bed.
Don't go round with them.
Along a road you'll be led,
that won't ever reach an end.'

Leaving Home

'Twas,
>there in a south-western town,
you would hear
a train whistle blowing.
Grew up dreaming, like all kids do,
wondering where
it was going?

Yeah,
>I grew up dreaming, like all kids do,
at the end of the railroad
lies my pot of gold.
In a part of my mind, that ribbon of steel
kept running through.
Though my momma was never told.

Born and raised,
>in that sou'-western town, just a kid
growing old from dreaming.
Listen to that train whistle blow.
If only I could ride that ribbon of steel,
to the places it has to go.
Momma just might lose her frown.

Yeah.

    I'd be hanging around
    day 'n' night,
    listening to stories
    those drivers would tell.
    Exciting tales of places seen,
    when they rode that ribbon of steel.
    Knew I had to see
    such a sight.

Go...

    Where those drivers have been.
    Something inside my head, made it swell.
    A voice saying, 'Come on, boy,
    you've gotta be northern-bound.'
    Growing up in a south-western town,
    didn't think like other kids,
    asking momma, why?

Yes,

    I've got a dream.
    It's riding that ribbon of steel.
    Momma packed my port.
    Poppa said, 'Take it easy, son,
    wherever you go.'

Me.
        Settled in my seat,
        Northern-bound.

'Twas,
        There in a sou'-western town,
        I grew up dreaming,
        wanting to follow those ribbons of steel,
        going wherever they take me,
        northern-bound.

You Don't Understand Him

He's gone down this highway, Momma,
just to find some peace of mind,
stepping out, a nagging doubt,
from that world left behind.

Pockets are empty,
always the same,
searching for another adventure to tame.

You don't understand him.
Guess you never will.
You have for so long been
listening to a crazy scheme,
stories told, how he's gonna be
a rich man some day.

He's gone down the highway, Momma,
one of a kind, travelling blind,
following his route – you've got a doubt,
glory-bound is only in his mind.

Pockets are empty,
always the same,
chasing another adventure to tame.

For you can't understand him,
guess you never will.
You want him to settle down
but he's duty-bound,
tryin' to prove, once 'n' for all,
fortune 'n' fame will come his way.

He stays upon the highway, Momma,
some way he knows milk 'n' honey flows.
In the distance given and earning a living,
he's gotta follow his heart wherever he goes.

Yes, pockets are empty,
isn't it the same,
when another adventure you tame.

Can you not understand him?
Guess you never will.
Open the mind, stop being blind.
There on his own, looking for a home,
is truthfully the way it's been,
as he wanders from day to day.

It's not so easy, Momma,
walking the highway, there to stay.
Fortune 'n' fame is just a name,
survival is the quest from an educated guess.

'Cos the pockets are empty,
isn't it the same.
As you find another adventure to tame.

A Letter Home

Dearest Mother and Father,
Here tonight I sit, with just a word or two,
saying your son is missing you.
I've been on the road travelling,
and time has a way of unravelling
a chance to settle down.

Been out upon those Queensland plains,
drifting along with the sunshine 'n' rains.
Been rodeoing, droving, breaking in horses.
These young stock I'm working, south of course,
along this Darling River and its watercourse.

Geez, you'd not think that I was seventeen.
Two long years, goin' to places never been.
Your note caught me on the Queensland side.
Been a while since towards a town I'd ride,
though your words help when I feel down.

This old bloke, Tom, knew you, Dad.
He told me stories of the horses you had.
Never knew, till now, you'd travelled around.
Now it seems you understand why I'm bound
upon this road of learning.

Miss you, Mum, with all my heart,
though sometimes I know why we part.
A man can't stay to apron strings,
though at night I think of things
that would've been if I wasn't northern-bound.

Old Bronc Saddle

Only legacy my Daddy left me,
was an old bronc saddle
and a pair of Willoughby spurs.
He gave me some good advice,
when I said I was goin'
down the road livin' free.
Told me that life would be a battle,
out in the ring, when the dust stirs.
But I didn't have to think twice.
It's the only legacy Daddy gave to me.

Saddle sittin' on the gate at Marrabelle.
Cowboy came up to me and said,
'Don't let that riggin' down, boy, I know it well.'
Then he asked how long Dad's been dead.
'Kinda been keepin' an eye out, boy,' he told me then.
''Cos of a promise to a friend.'
Yeah, he knew Daddy well.

Gave me a hand to screw her down.
Placed a hand upon my shakin' knee.
'With all the money we get today,
boy, we'll paint the town.'
It's wide and open, you see,
across that ring and you wonder what they'll say
when you come out of this livin' hell.

Hope they won't frown,
'cos they know this saddle well.
I won't let it down.

Only legacy my Daddy left me
was an old bronc saddle
and a pair of Willoughby spurs.
He gave me good advice,
when I said I was goin' down the road livin' free.
Told me life would be a battle,
out there in the ring, where the dust stirs.
But I didn't think twice.
It's the only legacy Daddy left me.

No Bed of Roses

'Twas in a northern cattle town,
where I landed as a kid.
Knocking about with ringers and such.
Oh, the things we did.
Soon taught me to grow up.
Hard lessons are what I found.

Growing old, so young,
is how I lived my dreams.
A full-grown man 'neath the sun,
proud of my Akubra hat 'n' longhorn jeans,
sitting the saddle of a sour-tempered horse.
Getting into trouble for things I hadn't done.
Sure was no bed of roses, of course.

North-western cattle camps,
days on end following sheep.
Along the roads, itchy feet tramp.
Lonely nights I wanted to sleep
with a roof over my head, not hungry or damp.
Feelings for my old sou'-western home ran deep.

Sometimes I could hear that train whistle blow.
Over many a year,
I had an urge to know.
Yes, like a kid my heart would feel
a mother's kind words, a father's handshake.
A southern port on the ribbon of steel,
going home, yarning to an old mate.

A Treasured Memory

I met him at the sale yards.
Just a kid, wasn't I?
Not long away from home,
doing the best, just to get by.
Just drifting, when others wouldn't leave alone.
Just someone wanting to give life a try.

He said, 'Boy are you looking for a job?
Can you ride?
Ain't afraid of a day's work?
Need a person to offside,
'cos I'm breakin' horses back o' Bourke.'
I hadn't much to hide.
Nothing in my jeans an' needing a new shirt.
Been around long enough not to show pride.

I was leaving behind yesterday,
ain't no good looking behind – it's been 'n' gone.
Got to look towards another way.
Tomorrow is another song,
that's the way it seems to me.
With this old feller, driftin' on,
life would be happy 'n' free.

Thirty horses we done on the Darling,
not too bad a mob, but on the flighty side.
Though the old feller had their measure,
never taking away their pride.
Watching, learning was a pleasure.
Said, 'Done the job well – good man at my side.'
Those words forever I will treasure.

Riding Broncs, Chasing Bulls

It's riding broncs and chasing bulls,
heading south, picking fruit.
Getting money for a hungry mouth and a drink
for my old ute.

Yeah I've been riding broncs and mustering
bulls, travelling a lot of miles playing this game.
Seen some good men come and go.
Pretty women with loving eyes,
chasing a dream to tame.

Yes, it's been a long time playing this game.
Had some luck at the country shows,
over-eager in my goodbyes,
Started out as a child,
bright-eyed over dreams to tame.
Like an animal in the wild,
had wings to spread and earn a name.

Parted home, leaving mum.
Needed space and the world is wide.
Grew up knowing I was different from some,
dreams no longer could hide.

For it's been riding broncs and chasing bulls,
travelling on for another song,
adding a name towards distant fame,
that's the only dream we tame.

On the Road of Rodeo

I pulled into this one-horse town,
a tired and thirsty bloke.
Haven't got a clue, old mate,
how long me throat's been dry.
I sure am glad this pub I've found,
and fair dinkum that's no joke.
Gonna take a well earned break,
that something to myself I won't deny.
Strike me pink. I need that drink,
and that's no lie.
Fair dinkum, mate, I'm telling you straight,
me throat is fairly dry.

Where am I from, what am I doing here,
you want to know.
'I'm just another cowboy
on the road of rodeo.
Just another ploughboy,
waiting for a star to grow.'

The beer was nice and cold.
But, strike me dead, this feller said,
'You ain't the usual mould.
Such a little feller to be led
upon the trail, chasing gold.'
From the tip of toe to top of me head,
in no uncertain terms he was told –
words like that and teeth he'd shed.

Strike me blue, I'm telling you,
I was gonna have him.
Yes, for a moment or two
life looked mighty grim.
Like a bantam chook, I had a look,
thought to myself, 'I'd better settle down.
For I'm just another ploughboy
on the road of rodeo.
Ain't no peace in this town.
They don't want me around.'

Boy from the Bush, Girl from Town

He stood out like a beacon on the hill,
a boy from the bush in town.
High-heeled boots upon his feet,
hat upon his unruly head.
Gave the pretty girls a thrill
when they saw him hanging round
this singles' bar where they all meet.
To each other they all said,

'Wonder who the cowboy is,
wonder if it's all true
wonder if they linger over a kiss,
like in the movies they do?'

One little lady with a heart of gold,
more impulsive than the rest,
picked up her glass of ale,
wandered over to where he sat.
Says she, 'Cowboy, I'm told
cowboys as lovers are the best.
Now, cowboy, is that a fact?'

'Stay beside me here tonight
and wander with me in the morning,
girl, I'll show you who is right
and you'll find new life dawning.'

Lonely Lady

She had red roses in her hair,
talked a lot about Queensland
and the cattle camps out there.
She asked me if Herman is shooting 'roos,
and does Dallas still use the Tabrah brand?
She was hungry for home-town news.
She was lonely, she was blue,
to the city she was new.
Finding work was hard to do,
hard to find someone true.

She talked a lot about lonely,
how tough life had been.
Going home would be nice if only
conscience was eased over what she had seen.

We rolled a swag out by the river,
each holding on, for fear meant another day
and another lonely night.
Thinking of her leaving gave me a shiver,
as we made love in the moonlight.
Love was ours to share and deliver.

She talked a lot about lonely,
how tough life had been.
Going home would be nice if only
conscience was eased over what she'd seen.

Two Lonely People

Serious were the words meant,
as I took her hands,
those lovely work-hardened hands.
Idle chatter over time spent,
for we had a lifetime to recall.

She pondered over children gone,
while I talked of roads travelled.
There was yesterday's dreams,
                today's schemes,
                and tomorrow's.

Oh yes, there's always tomorrow.

She sat and listened all night long.
Laughter came easy as we talked,
entertaining each other's loneliness
as we rolled back the years.
Friendship created challenges, we'd seen.
It was but a moment in time,
a moment in time, we walked.

Money Lost Or Won

Today is over and done.
>We'll get movin' on
>with money lost or won.

Yeah,
>with money lost or won.

Friends, you laughed at the clown,
groaned when that young cowboy
went falling down.
Could you know, or even understand,
while you sat down and enjoyed,
the guts of what was done?
That boy's travelling across the land
on money lost or won.

Yeah, the dust settles down on a small country town,
today is over and done.
>We'll get movin' on with money lost or won.

Yeah,
>with money lost or won.

Travel the Gravel

Towns don't like you, mister.
You better get goin', movin' on.
Towns don't need you, mister.
Bums like you are better off gone.

Bums, I suppose you could say,
in town for your pleasure.
And, yes, we like to play
and true freedom we treasure.

Shake my hand and call me mate,
Take my money and pat my back.
To your friends you state,
'You're doing a favour for a fool on the track.'

There in the bar room,
abounding with noise.
Camp on the showgrounds.
'Yes, I'm one of the boys.'

Come the end of the rodeo,
it's another song.
It's easy to mistake me, don't I know,
for the town doesn't need me and it shows.
Yes, with happiness I'll be moving on.
I'm just another saddle bum, better off gone.

So it's travel the gravel,
see another place, hope it's fine.
Luck on your side and a mystery to unravel.
Maybe this is the moment, giving you the time
to loosen the girth on a worn-out saddle.

It's gather your saddle and worn swag.
Catch a Greyhound bus, rodeo-bound.
Fast we travel the gravel.

Sleeping easy by a rivergum fire,
drinking whisky or rum and taking whatever comes,
that's all a loner can desire.

So it's travel the gravel,
see another place, hope it's fine.
Luck on your side and a mystery to unravel.
Maybe this is the moment, giving you the time
to loosen the girth on a worn-out saddle.

Stray Dog Like Me

I'm going down to Casey's
listen to a country song.
Hey there, women,
can't you see,
I'm a new boy in town?
Won't you take my blues away?
Ain't got time for foolin' 'round,
I'm just a bad dog gotta stray.
Yeah, I'm a bad dog
gotta stray.

Seen a mile of highway blues
smell of country air and cattle camps.
Long of hair and called a tramp,
been a while since I read the news.
Really, what would people know?
I'm a country boy,
grown man wherever I go.

Busted flat in a game of chance,
lost my head and can't recall my mind.
Losing weight and need new pants.
City friend, I'm not your kind.
Give me another saddle to ride,
know it's time to gather my pride.

Came into your pasture for a time —
concrete fields and lonely nights.
Fell for a false smile,
going crazy, gotta fight.
Girl, can't you see,
what it's doing to me?

Walking around this city street,
lonely as a man could ever be.
Searching for another to meet —
someone like me.

Life Upon the Road

There's a truck stop where you'll find
yourself bed 'n' breakfast and a dinkum decent deal.
It's there for us to share,
we that are one of a kind.
A moment or two to steal,
and an ear that really cares.

There's a pub where time stands still,
and all are welcome guests.
It's home to many a soul,
where you can try your yarning skill.
Your name is known. There's respect,
whenever you come in from the cold.

There's a shaded waterhole,
a creek where water is clean.
Good burning mallee, that we seek,
as you listen to stories told
of different places, where others have been,
plenty of wood, clean country where we can sleep.

There's places to camp,
roads that travel on,
people who are a wanderer's friend
as across this land we tramp,
miles made lonely and long.
Some day in paradise they'll end.

Rodeo Is What I Gotta Do

Told by the doctor yesterday,
gotta give the broncs away.
Feel kinda funny,
getting eating money,
bumming around this old town.

I've tried my luck on ones that buck,
and those that twist and turn,
I've chanced my style to a pretty girl's smile,
but the open road I'll always yearn.

I'm bumming around this old town,
not the life for a gypsy like me.
Gonna get a saddle ride tomorrow.
Sweet little girl, don't you see,
wishing well won't fix the sorrow.

Told by the doctor yesterday,
have to give the broncs away.
Left my childhood far behind,
had this thing on my mind.

I've tried my luck on those that buck,
and those that twist and turn,
Chanced my style to a pretty girl's smile,
and the right I'd earn.
Living free, doing what has to be.

Found a bar where dreams abound,
aloud for all to see,
but the grog won't drown
what's happening to me.

Gonna try my luck on those that buck,
and those that twist and turn,
Chance my style to a pretty girl's smile,
try to give in return
what I've seen for a while.

'Cos the doctor told me yesterday,
'Give the dreams away.'
Tried to explain
how I love the game.

You've gotta try your luck,
on the ones that buck,
the moments that twist and turn.
You chance your style to a pretty girl's smile.
What else is there we can learn?

Rodeo Widow

She walks to the homestead door.
Rising glow in the east says, 'Good morning.'
She walks out to the stockyard gate
and catches a horse that's not too poor.

There's cattle need tending in the furthest field.
Noontime is gonna be hot.
Through the rising of sunrise and dust,
tired arms and faded dreams, the stockwhip wields
the plight of what she's got.

For she's a rodeo widow, her man's gone.
He's gone away, riding broncs and chasing bulls,
trying to earn a dollar so she can carry on.

There's water in the lower forty acres still.
Not much feed, but a drink is a drink.
Take them easy now, don't take the chance.
You haven't the heart for a mercy kill,
and what would he say or think?
Was it yesterday he drove out of sight?
Wonder when he'll have time to call?
Dreaming alone is hardest most
when lying in bed at night.
For she's a rodeo widow, having doubts
whether she'll survive this land,
while fighting this blasted drought.

The Aussie Battlers' Hymn

Dusty boots upon his feet,
money in the pocket of jeans faded blue,
getting by with enough to eat.
A battling man an' that's true.

You can laugh and wonder why?
Seven days and chasing dreams,
workin' hard and another time to try.
Riches are there, out of reach it seems.

Worn old hat covers his face.
Needin' rain to sow the wheat.
When luck was given, he lost the race,
but you'll never see him beat.

You can laugh and wonder why?
Seven days and chasin' dreams,
workin' hard and another time to try.
Riches are there, out of reach it seems.

Sweat stains on his flannel shirt,
limps a little from carrying a load.
Keeps on going, even feeling hurt,
'cos it's in the genes his father sowed.

You can laugh and wonder why?
Seven days and chasing dreams,
workin' hard and another time to try.
Riches are there, out of reach it seems.

He's made the money others reap,
fought the wars with drought 'n' flood,
given joy to a love that weeps,
when his time is done from sweat 'n' blood.

You can laugh and wonder why?
Seven days and chasin' dreams,
workin' hard and another time to try.
Riches are there – out of reach, it seems.

Keeping the Wolf from the Door

I started life with a dream.
Working hard, I'd gather rewards,
but…
here I stand an angry man,
wondering where my money went.
Now then, mister, I got to say,
this hard-earned money spent
trying to keep our head above water.
Yeah…
trying to keep our head above water.

It's been me and a good man's daughter,
whose daddy told her, when she got older,
someone will come along,
carry her down the aisle in a stately style.
Yeah…
gonna keep her in a stately style.

But we battle and curse all the while,
and now I've got something to say:
'It was going to be easy, this game to play.'
But…
we never knew we'd only be keeping
the wolf from the door.
Yeah, keeping the wolf from the door.

A Woman at Home

He climbs into the cabin, blows the horn,
and rolls down the highway.
The music on the wireless tells a story of love gone wrong.
It's only a sad country song. But Bill thinks of Mary,
waiting at home.
He has the mobile phone and CB radio in the truck.
He knows he's only twenty-three miles up the road from home.
'I'll ring her now,' says he. He's sure he told her he
loved her, but he's got an interstate trip and who knows
when he'll be home?

'Sweetheart,
It's only me, Bill.
Just thought I'd say, "I love you."
No, darl,
I'm not getting crook or anything else.
Been popping pills.
Just wanted to say something:
this is gonna be a long trip.'

She hangs up the phone and thinks about him.
It's all she's got: Bill and the kids.
Monday. Home on Thursday.
No good standing around moping –
clothes to hang out, kids to feed.
But she's lucky, her man loves her.
That's all she needs.

Rest of the time,
she'll go on coping – or hoping.

Haven't Lost My Dreams

I look out my window
as another day passes by.
It would be good, you know,
if I could hear the wind sigh
and feel the cool breeze blow.
No matter where we go,
it's not easy to live a lie.

'Twas lonely nights singing the blues,
good days on the open roads.
Luck of the draw is the news,
as we carried a heavy load.
Goodbyes as we passed through.
In a hurry, life was slowed.

Yes, slowed when struck a tree,
trying to beat the hands of time.
Here tonight, you can see,
those wasted legs that are mine.
Looking out the window, can't go free,
that's the luck that'll bind,
travelling through me.
Now, don't feel unkind.

Country songs and wishing well,
someone uncomfortable it seems.
In your heart I can tell,
talking, made hard by means,
you only make the hurt swell.
Don't go thinking I've lost my dreams.

A Lost Soul

He sits in the corner every day,
upon a bar stool that he claims.
Don't go near him, *mister*, that's the loser's hot spot.
Across the room the jukebox will play
and, around us, pool is the game.
But the moment you see him, *sister*,
you'll know what you've got.

It's drink another glass and then
he will tell you a story, when
he looks back on glory,
over what he has done.

So he sits in the bar room by day,
in that corner he calls his own.
No more does he seek a job,
or hold a woman to his chest,
feeling like it's his part to play,
forgoing the safety of a home.
Lost and deprived from the everyday mob,
nothing does he see in jest.

He seldom talks to another,
or seeks to be a friend.
The rest of the world may roll
but he remembers a lover
and wonders why it had to end.
For he's just a shadow…a lost soul.

www.ingramcontent.com/pod-product-compliance
Lightning Source LLC
Chambersburg PA
CBHW062207100526
44589CB00014B/1988